WOMEN IN SCIENCE

MAE JEMISON

Awesome Astronaut

Jill C. Wheeler

ABDO Publishing Company

visit us at
www.abdopublishing.com

Published by ABDO Publishing Company, PO Box 398166, Minneapolis, MN 55439. Copyright © 2013 by Abdo Consulting Group, Inc. International copyrights reserved in all countries. No part of this book may be reproduced in any form without written permission from the publisher. The Checkerboard Library™ is a trademark and logo of ABDO Publishing Company.

Printed in the United States of America, North Mankato, Minnesota.
052012
092012

 PRINTED ON RECYCLED PAPER

Cover Photos: Getty Images; courtesy of NASA
Interior Photos: AP Images pp. 13, 17; Corbis pp. 15, 21, 23, 25; Getty Images pp. 5, 9, 18, 24, 27; iStockphoto p. 11; courtesy of NASA pp. 7, 19

Series Coordinator: BreAnn Rumsch
Editors: Tamara L. Britton, BreAnn Rumsch
Art Direction: Neil Klinepier

Library of Congress Cataloging-in-Publication Data

Wheeler, Jill C., 1964-
  Mae Jemison: awesome astronaut / Jill C. Wheeler.
      p. cm. -- (Women in science)
  Includes index.
  ISBN 978-1-61783-447-9
  1. Jemison, Mae, 1956---Juvenile literature. 2. African American women astronauts--Biography--Juvenile literature. 3. Astronauts--United States--Biography--Juvenile literature. I. Title.
  TL789.85.J46W43 2012
  629.450092--dc23
  [B]
                                    2012004885

CONTENTS

MAE JEMISON

"Don't let anyone rob you of your imagination, your creativity, or your curiosity. It's your place in the world; it's your life. Go on and do all you can with it, and make it the life you want to live."

— *Mae Jemison*

Mae Jemison is the first African-American woman to travel into space. Yet this is just one reason she is a role model. She is also a successful doctor and business owner.

Jemison grew up wanting to be a scientist. But during her childhood, few women had careers in science. And no people of color worked as **astronauts**. Jemison refused to believe she could not make her dream come true. Her determination led her to join the US **Space Shuttle** Program.

Jemison thinks science is simply about wanting to know why things are the way they are. She says finding those answers should be open to anyone. So today, Jemison inspires young people of all backgrounds to think about careers in science.

DREAMING BIG

 In 1993, Mae appeared in an episode of Star Trek: The Next Generation called "Second Chances."

Mae Carol Jemison was born October 17, 1956, in Decatur, Alabama. Her father, Charlie Jemison, was a roofer and carpenter. Her mother, Dorothy Green Jemison, was an elementary school teacher. Mae was their youngest child. She had a brother named Ricky and a sister named Ada Sue.

When Mae was three years old, the Jemisons moved to Chicago, Illinois. In Chicago, young Mae watched the **Gemini space missions** on television. She also watched Star Trek. She wished she had some of the cool gadgets used on the show!

On the show, the crew came from all over the world. Mae liked that Lieutenant Uhura was a woman from Africa. Uhura helped Mae believe she could someday travel to space, too.

One time in kindergarten, Mae's teacher asked her what she wanted to be when she grew up. Mae quickly replied, "A scientist." At the time, scientists were mostly men. So the teacher said, "Don't you mean a nurse?" But Mae knew she wanted to be a scientist!

Nichelle Nichols played Star Trek*'s Lieutenant Uhura. Nichols was the first African-American actress to play a scientist on television.*

ACADEMIC STAR

>> *In her free time, Mae loved to dance. She started taking dance lessons when she was eight years old.*

Growing up, Mae was an excellent student. She also spent a lot of time at the library. Mae often walked there and read about space and science.

At home, Mae conducted her own science experiments. Once, she made mud pies and put flowers on them. She wanted to find out if the flowers would keep growing. Mae's parents supported her curiosity. They helped her find the answers to her questions.

All through elementary school, Mae entered science fairs. One project lasted for several years. It was called Eras of Time. It allowed her to study prehistoric animals such as dinosaurs and giant sloths.

In July 1969, Mae watched Apollo 11 on television. The mission featured **astronauts** Neil Armstrong, Michael Collins, and Edwin "Buzz" Aldrin. Armstrong and Aldrin were the first humans to walk on the moon! After this, Mae read everything she could about the mission.

Mae's interest in science was still strong when she entered Morgan Park High School. At age 15, her science fair project took her to a local hospital. There, she learned about **sickle cell anemia**. She helped test a way to treat this disease.

As a grown-up, Mae likes to share her love of space with kids around the world.

EXPLORING SCIENCE

Jemison graduated from high school in 1973. Her good grades earned her a National Achievement **Scholarship**. With it, she entered Stanford University near Palo Alto, California.

Jemison knew she wanted a career in science. Yet, she also wanted to learn more about her **culture**. So, she studied **chemical engineering** as well as African and African-American studies.

Jemison's focus on science meant many hours of studying! But she still found time for other interests. Jemison took dance classes and performed in several plays. She also led the Black Student Union.

It didn't take long for Jemison to see that women in science still faced **discrimination**. One day, she asked a question in class. The professor looked at Jemison as if she were stupid.

Later, a white male in the class asked the same question. The professor admired this student! This different treatment caused Jemison to question herself. Still, she was determined to succeed.

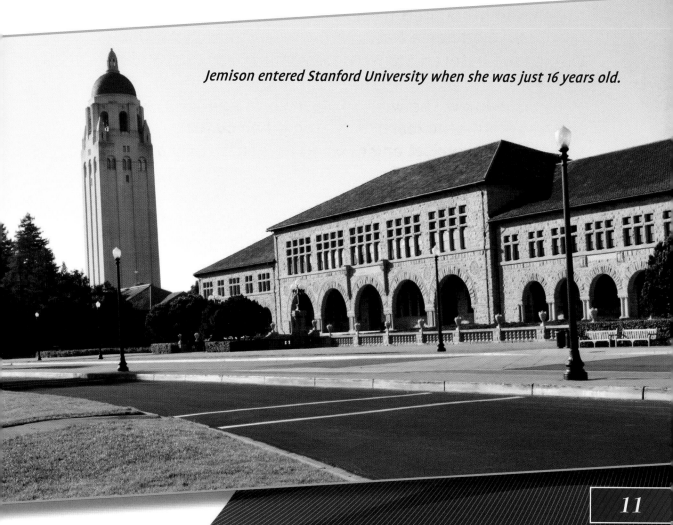

Jemison entered Stanford University when she was just 16 years old.

LEARNING AND SERVING

Jemison graduated from Stanford in 1977. She decided to continue her education and become a doctor. Jemison was accepted to Cornell Medical College. She moved to New York City, New York, to begin school.

For four years, Jemison studied medicine. However, not all of that time was spent in classrooms in New York. She went to Cuba with a group of medical students. She also traveled to Africa. There, she worked with the Flying Doctors in Kenya. This program operates an air ambulance service.

Jemison also spent time in a **refugee** camp in Thailand. Jemison later said she learned more about medicine there than she could have learned anywhere else. She feels she received more in experience than she gave in service.

At Cornell, Jemison was one of just four African-American women in her class of 105 students.

DR. JEMISON

 Jemison is fluent in several languages. She can speak English, Russian, Japanese, and Swahili!

In 1981, Jemison graduated from medical school. She returned to California for her **internship**. She worked at the Los Angeles County/University of Southern California Medical Center.

Jemison completed this work in July 1982. For the next few months, she stayed in Los Angeles working as a doctor. But in January 1983, she returned to Africa.

Jemison had volunteered to join the **Peace Corps**. She spent two and a half years in Sierra Leone and Liberia. There, Jemison worked as a medical officer. She finished her service in June 1985.

After Jemison returned to the United States, she again worked as a doctor in California. But the break in traveling would not last long! Soon, Jemison would get the chance to fulfill her childhood dream.

Jemison hard at work in LA

SHOOTING FOR THE STARS

>> *During NASA's 30-year Space Shuttle Program, 306 men and 49 women flew aboard shuttles.*

In the mid-1980s, the National Aeronautics and Space Administration (NASA) was accepting new candidates to train as **astronauts**.

Jemison had considered joining the training program before. However, it had not always been open to women and people of color. Yet in 1978, Sally Ride had been accepted. So, Jemison now felt she stood a better chance.

Still, getting accepted was not easy! Astronauts had to be in good shape. They needed strong scientific skills. And they had to be able to handle the **stress** of space travel. Jemison believed she fit these requirements. So in November 1985, she applied to the program.

At NASA, training equipment is often just like the real thing!

On January 28, 1986, Jemison was waiting for NASA's response. But that day, the **space shuttle** *Challenger* exploded. As a result, NASA officials put off any decisions on the training program applications.

Jemison remained patient. In fall 1986, she tried applying again. Finally, Jemison was asked to travel to Houston, Texas. There, officials asked her questions and ran medical tests.

On June 4, 1987, good news made the wait worthwhile. Jemison was one of just 15 people chosen from more than 2,000! She was the first African-American woman ever accepted into the training program.

*Houston, Texas, is home to NASA's
Johnson Space Center.*

19

ASTRONAUT TRAINING

Jemison's childhood dream of being an **astronaut** was finally coming true. Her journey into space began in August 1987 with a move to Houston, Texas. Jemison joined the other astronaut candidates at NASA's Johnson Space Center. There, they trained and prepared for future missions.

Astronauts rarely know in advance to which mission they will be assigned. They are also unsure when it will take place. Their first year focuses on preparing for life in space.

During this time, Jemison and the others learned about the effects of space on the body and mind. They practiced moving around in zero-gravity **environments**. They also had to learn what to do in case there was an emergency while they were in space.

After her first year of training, Jemison became a Science-Mission Specialist. For this assignment, Jemison spent additional time training in Japan.

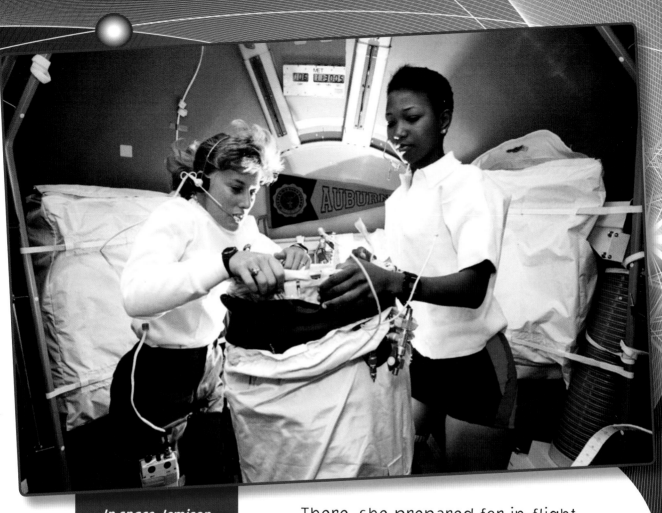

There, she prepared for in-flight experiments she would conduct. Some of the experiments would observe how space affected the crew. Jemison's medical training made her a perfect fit for her new job.

EIGHT AMAZING DAYS

>> *Jemison describes* Endeavour's *blastoff feeling like sitting on top of a controlled explosion.*

After years of preparation, Jemison's training came to an end on September 12, 1992. She and six other **astronauts** traveled to Kennedy Space Center in Cape Canaveral, Florida. There, they boarded the **space shuttle** *Endeavour*.

It blasted off from the launchpad at 10:23 AM. The astronauts were thrust into space at 17,500 miles per hour (28,160 kph)!

The crew was beginning mission STS-47. NASA teamed up with Japan's National Space Development Agency for STS-47. The astronauts would spend eight days in space and travel 3.3 million miles (5.3 million km).

During STS-47, the crew conducted nearly 50 experiments. Jemison was in charge of some of them. She observed and recorded what happens to people when they are weightless. She paid special attention to the effects of zero gravity on human bone cells.

Jemison also experimented with frogs. She hatched tadpoles from frog eggs for the experiment. She studied how they developed without gravity.

Jemison continued to monitor them when *Endeavour* returned to Earth. From her work, Jemison concluded that tadpoles do not develop differently in space.

Working in the space lab aboard Endeavour was tricky without gravity!

NEW CHALLENGES

After STS-47, Jemison was honored for her role as the first African-American woman in space. She used this fame to make a difference. She stated that women and people of color had much to offer.

Jemison also had a decision to make. She had no idea when she might return to space. It could be soon, or it could be years. Did she want to wait? In March 1993, Jemison announced she was leaving NASA. It was a hard choice to make. But, there were more challenges that Jemison wanted to take on.

Shortly after leaving NASA, Jemison got started on one of them. She set up a company called the Jemison

The Endeavour *crew returned to Earth on September 20, 1992.*

Group. The company focused on solving problems in developing nations with new technology.

One of the company's first projects was to use **satellites** for communication in West Africa. Jemison and her team improved how health workers there could share information.

Some people believe Jemison is one of several American women most likely to become US president.

SCIENCE SUPPORTER

In 1994, Jemison launched a science camp called the Earth We Share. At the camp, kids ages 12 to 16 learn how to solve problems with activities and experiments.

Then in 1999, Jemison started a second company called BioSentient Corporation. It develops special medical devices. Doctors use them to monitor patients during real-life activities.

It wasn't long before Jemison also began working with the children's program Making Science Make Sense. Jemison says children are natural scientists. They are always asking why things are the way they are. That is the heart of science, she says.

In 2009, Jemison partnered with First Lady Michelle Obama. She spoke to students about following their dreams and staying in school. Then in 2011, Jemison returned to her dream of space travel. She joined a special project supported by NASA. Its goal is to develop the first starship within 100 years!

In 1995, Jemison began teaching at Dartmouth College in Hanover, New Hampshire. Today, she enjoys speaking to and inspiring students of all ages.

Mae Jemison hopes her work will take some of the mystery out of science for children of color and all girls. Anyone can be a scientist, Jemison says. All it takes is curiosity!

TIMELINE

1956	**1973**	**1977**	**1981**	**1983**	**1987**
On October 17, Mae Carol Jemison was born in Decatur, Alabama.	Mae graduated from Morgan Park High School in Chicago, Illinois.	Jemison graduated from Stanford University near Palo Alto, California.	Jemison graduated from Cornell Medical College in New York City, New York.	Jemison joined the Peace Corps to serve in Africa.	On June 4, Jemison became the first African-American woman accepted into NASA's astronaut training program.

1992	**1993**	**1994**	**1999**	**2009**	**2011**
On September 12, Jemison launched into space aboard the space shuttle *Endeavour*.	Jemison decided to leave NASA and start the Jemison Group.	Jemison started a science camp for kids called the Earth We Share.	Jemison launched BioSentient Corporation.	Jemison joined First Lady Michelle Obama's effort to encourage students to follow their dreams.	Jemison joined a special space project to help develop the first starship.

DIG DEEPER

As an astronaut, Dr. Mae Jemison understood the importance of gravity. This force keeps us from floating off into space! On Earth, every object feels gravity's pull. The part of the object that feels the strongest pull weighs the most. This is the object's center of gravity. Now check out a fun way to observe this force at work!

SUPPLIES:
• a 12-inch (30-cm) wooden ruler • 12 inches (30 cm) of cotton twine • a hammer

INSTRUCTIONS: *Always ask an adult for help!*

1 Balance the ruler on your index finger. Do this by resting the flat side of the ruler's center point on your finger. It balances because your finger is at the ruler's center of gravity. So, gravity's pull is equal on either side of the ruler.

2 Tie the cotton twine in a loop. Place one end of the ruler on a table, leaving most of its length extended out beyond the table's edge. Hold the ruler in place on the tabletop with your hand. Place the loop of twine on the other end of the ruler. Let the twine hang down toward the floor.

3 Put the hammer's head through the loop of twine. The handle should rest against the ruler. The head should hang underneath the table.

4 Now lift your hand off the ruler. The ruler should no longer need your help to stay balanced! Based on what you know about gravity, why do you think that is? Next, observe how rulers and hammers of different sizes change the structure's center of gravity.

GLOSSARY

astronaut – a person who is trained to travel into outer space.

chemical engineering – a branch of engineering that applies chemistry for industrial uses. Chemistry is a science that studies substances and the changes they go through.

culture – the customs, arts, and tools of a nation or a people at a certain time.

discrimination – unfair treatment, often based on race, religion, or gender.

environment – all the surroundings that affect the growth and well-being of a living thing.

Gemini space missions – missions launched between 1962 and 1966 to send people into Earth's orbit.

internship – a program that allows a student or graduate to gain guided practical experience in a professional field.

Peace Corps – a body of trained volunteers sent to assist developing nations.

refugee – a person who flees to another country for safety and protection.

satellite - a manufactured object that orbits Earth. It relays scientific information back to Earth.

scholarship - money or aid given to help a student continue his or her studies.

sickle cell anemia - a disease in which red blood cells become crescent shaped. This sickling blocks blood flow in the body.

space shuttle - a reusable spacecraft designed to transport people and cargo between Earth and space.

stress - strain or pressure.

WEB SITES

To learn more about Mae Jemison, visit ABDO Publishing Company online. Web sites about Mae Jemison are featured on our Book Links page. These links are routinely monitored and updated to provide the most current information available.

www.abdopublishing.com

INDEX